Clare Johnson

HOW TO Draw

Design your own cover ↗

To design your cover, turn the page and fold out the flap.

DK

Contents

Let's go!

Design your very own
book cover HERE . . .

. . .then fold
the flap back.

DK

Draw a dangerous dinosaur!

Practice drawing a parrot!

Create and color in a cat!

Keep turning!

A note just for you!

Do you like drawing or think you'd like to try, but don't know where to start? Pick up this book for some inspiring ideas. It is packed with fun and easy suggestions to help you draw animals, people, places, and cartoons, with plenty of space to try out your own ideas too!

At the start of the book are four pages on **DRAWING TOOLS**—from pencils and pens to crayons and chalks.

STEP-BY-STEPS show you how to draw everything from your best friend to a fiery dragon. Pick up a pencil and get drawing!

FEATURE PAGES show basic ideas about drawing, from how things are arranged on the page to how to use color to show moods.

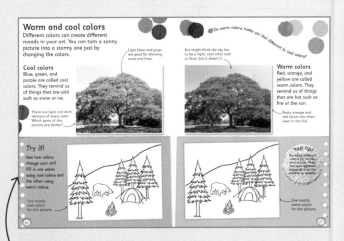

TOP TIPS give lots of hints and tricks to make your drawing better!

TRY IT! spaces appear throughout for you to try out different ideas.

Packed with lots of fresh new ideas to encourage budding artists!

At the end of the book, there are pages for drawing whatever you wish. It doesn't really matter what you draw, the important thing is to **HAVE FUN** with your drawing!

Pencils and pens

Pencils are a basic tool of drawing, but what else do you like to draw with? Here are some different types of pencils and pens to help get you started!

Felt-tip pens

You can color in your drawings using felt-tip pens, which are great for adding bold, bright colors.

Pencils

Pencils can be hard or soft. The softer the pencil, the darker the line it makes. Pencils are given letters and numbers that tell you how hard or soft they are.

Graphite pencils work on most kinds of paper except shiny paper.

6B (very soft) makes darker, smudgy lines

B (soft) makes dark, gray lines

3H (medium hard) makes sharp, light lines

6H (very hard) makes very light lines

Colored pencils

Pressing harder or softer with colored pencils changes the brightness of the colors.

If you press hard, colored pencils can show up well on most colored paper, too.

Rubber erasers rub away pencil marks.

Felt-tips can have a thick tip that is perfect for coloring big areas. A thin tip is best for small details.

Different tip sizes can be used for thicker or thinner lines.

These pens are especially good for drawing outlines and details.

Drawing pens
These pens are great for clear, sharp lines. People who draw cartoons and comics use these.

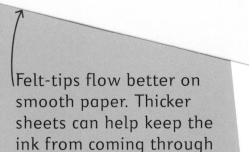

Felt-tips flow better on smooth paper. Thicker sheets can help keep the ink from coming through the other side of the paper.

You can use different pens and pencils for each project, or mix and match!

Fine drawing pens are great to use on smooth paper.

Digital art
When drawing on a tablet, you can choose from many different tools. They can be thick, thin, or even textured like spray paint.

Digital tools look like real pens and pencils, which you can use to fill color in digitally.

Crayons and pastels

Pastel sticks and crayons are great for adding color to your drawings. You can get all kinds of effects with these tools.

Chalk pastels

Chalk pastels are powdery and smudge easily. They can be soft and crumbly, so you don't need to press hard!

Oil pastels

Oil pastels are soft and sticky. They're messy, but great for mixing or adding layers of color.

It's best to use thick paper with oil pastels because the oil can come through the paper.

Conté crayons

These colored sticks are made of wax and chalk to make drawing easier and smoother.

Conté crayons do not smudge as much as chalk pastels because of the wax in them.

Oil pastels make thick marks packed with color.

6

You can use your finger or a bit of tissue to smear and blend chalk.

Crayons

Wax crayons are easy to use but do not blend together like pastels.

Crayons are great on any paper.

Kneaded erasers are sticky, to rub away marks from powdery tools like chalks and charcoal.

Charcoal

Charcoal is usually made from burned wood. It can be tricky to use at first, and can get messy, but it is great for shading.

Charcoal makes black or gray marks and smudges like chalk.

Top tip!

You can get a lovely soft look with charcoal by rubbing the charcoal mark with a cotton swab.

Drawing lines

You can draw lines in all sorts of ways. They can be thin or thick, smooth and steady, or rough and wiggly. They can be long and flowing, or short and broken up. Lines might be straight for buildings or wavy for rivers.

Straight

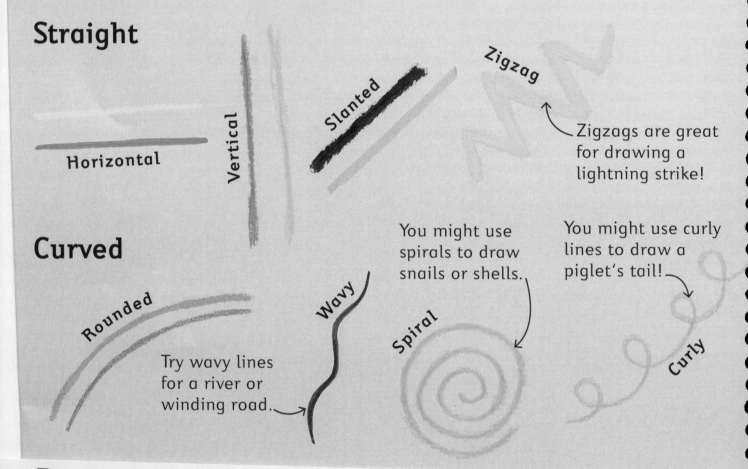

Horizontal

Vertical

Slanted

Zigzag

Zigzags are great for drawing a lightning strike!

Curved

Rounded

Try wavy lines for a river or winding road.

Wavy

You might use spirals to draw snails or shells.

Spiral

You might use curly lines to draw a piglet's tail!

Curly

Pressing down

Lines can be firm or soft, thick or thin depending on the type of pencil or pen you use, and how hard you press.

You can make your pencil lines fade away by smudging or using an eraser.

If the pastel is pressed lightly on the paper, the marks will be softer and lighter.

To make a thinner line, only touch the smallest part of a marker's tip to the paper.

Pencil

Oil pastel

Felt-tip pen

Dots and dashes

Dots and dashes are one way of making your drawing look softer, such as showing a floaty cloud. They are also great for showing movement.

Dots

Dashes

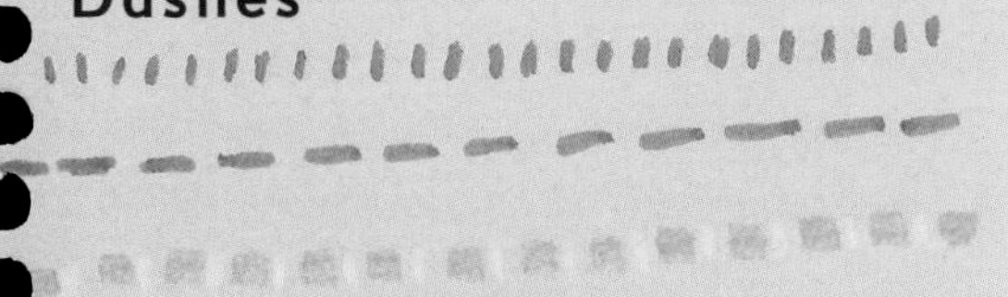

Broken lines around an object might be used to show it's shaking.

Dotted, wavy line

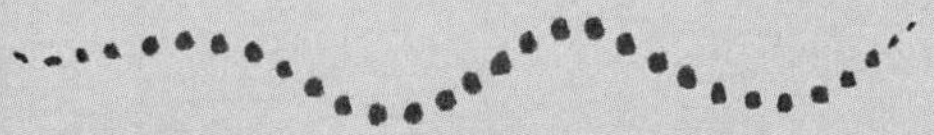

Dotted, zigzag line

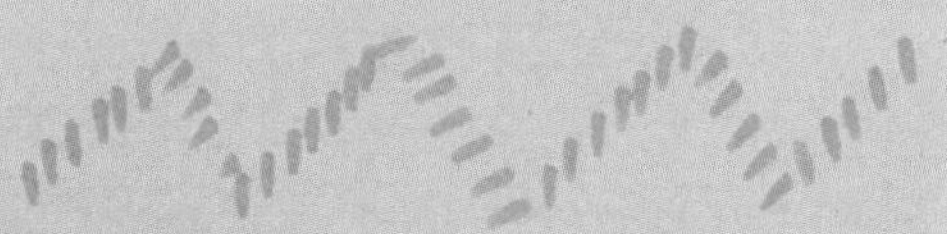

You might use a broken zigzag line to draw a partly-hidden path in a forest.

Top tip!

Lines can express feelings. Gentle, light lines can feel calm, while faster, bold lines might show excitement.

Try it!

How many different kinds of lines can you make? What type of lines would you use to draw a rough, rocky mountain, or smooth and delicate flower petals?

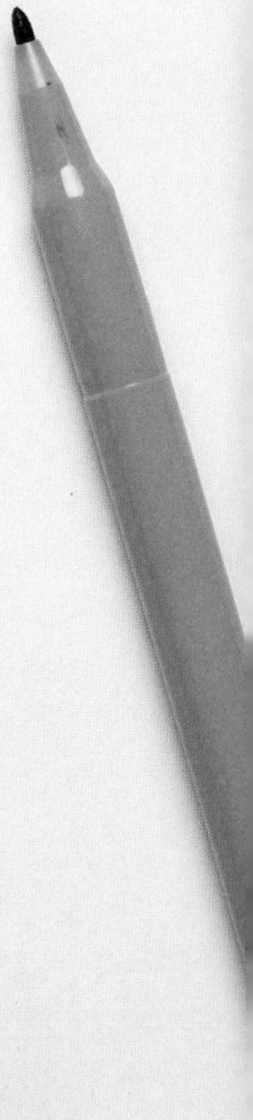

Drawing outlines

When you draw an outline of something you show its shape. Once you have your outline, you can fill it in with lots of colors and shading.

Drawing people

Stick figures are easy to draw, but outlining means you can add more detail.

With a stick figure, there's not much to color in.

Outlines look more real and let you color in all the details.

These sunrays are outlines, not just lines, so they can be filled with bright yellow.

You can make outlines in different colors. If you fill in with the same color, the outline disappears.

Shapes can be a good starting point. What shapes do you see in this house?

Outlines of the bushes use lots of small, bendy curves.

A wiggly, pointy outline shows spiky grass.

You can use thick, solid lines for firmer outlines.

You can outline in one color, and fill in with a different one for contrast.

Try it!

How would you outline the objects in these photos? The first one is started for you. Look to see where lines bend, get pointy, or make shapes such as the triangles in the sailing boat.

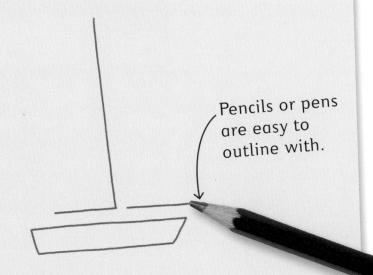

Pencils or pens are easy to outline with.

Leafy outlines

This drawing shows all the tree's leaves individually.

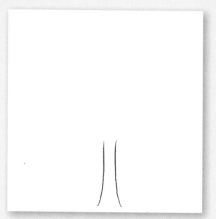

1 Draw two curved lines for the trunk, starting wider at the bottom.

2 Add branches spreading out from the top of the trunk.

You can add leaves to the spaces in between the branches, too.

3 Outline as many leaves as you can and then color your picture in. Try using different shades of green and brown.

Drawing trees

Here are two different ways to draw a tree. One has detailed leaves, while the other outlines the puffy shape of the whole tree.

Puffy outlines

This drawing outlines the shape of the whole area of leaves instead.

1 Draw a wiggly outline showing the leaves as a group.

2 Draw the trunk and branches disappearing into the leaves.

Trees have so many overlapping leaves that they can all blend together.

3 Color in the leaf area and trunk. Leave space to show the branches poking through the leaves.

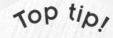

Top tip!
Start with your outlines, then add color. Think about how leaves can change color in different seasons.

Patterns

If you look around you, you can see patterns everywhere. Patterns are shapes that repeat, such as checks or stripes. You can see patterns in nature—in animal fur, butterfly wings, or on plant leaves. You'll also see them at home—on fabrics, wrapping paper, or buildings.

Spots

Checks

Stripes

Spotted patterns can be dots that are all the same size or speckles that vary in size, such as on this frog.

Checks are made up of lines that cross each other. The lines can vary in thickness. Compare this check to the pattern on the scarf.

Stripes can be straight or curvy such as on this fish.

Patterns look different depending on what they're on. What do the deck chair's stripes look like—are they straight or curved?

14

Try it!

Try drawing a favorite pattern that you might add onto wrapping paper. You might draw big spots, tiny dots, wide checks, or thick or thin stripes. Or try mixing and matching!

Top tip!

Draw simple shapes such as circles or triangles, then build on them and add flowers, animals, or anything you like!

Shapes can be inspired from the things around you or from your imagination!

How does it feel?

Texture is how something feels to touch, such as soft fur or rough concrete. You can use patterns, such as lines or dots, to show texture and make your drawings spring to life.

Scaly snake

Diamond shapes make a snakeskin pattern.

Fluffy toy

Short, gently curved lines drawn close together make this fur look soft and fluffy.

Fun with texture!

Here are a few ways of drawing different kinds of textures.

Rough tree bark

Use curvy, wiggly lines to show where an elephant's skin folds and wrinkles.

Tree bark has lines that change from smooth to jagged.

Grainy sand

Clusters of small dots make sand look grainy.

Wrinkly elephant

Spiky cactus

Draw cactus spikes as straight, skinny lines.

Try it!

Fill in the shapes with textures. What kinds of pens, pencils, or pastels do you think would be fun for drawing scaly, wrinkly, or spiky textures?

Top tip!

Try putting a piece of paper over some bark or a leaf. Coloring over the top of it will reveal its texture.

How to draw shells

If you look at shells on the seashore, you will see that they have different shapes, sizes, patterns, and textures. Here are two types of shell for you to draw.

Here are the grooves on the shell.

Fan-shaped shell

These shells come in pairs and they join together with a hinge. Sea creatures such as scallops and clams live in fan-shaped shells.

1 Draw straight lines for the hinged part of the shell, like three sides of a rectangle.

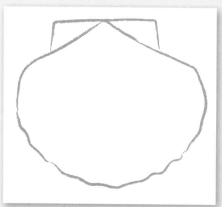

2 Add two lines from the middle of the hinge. Connect them with a wiggly curve.

3 Draw some straight lines from the curved edge to the central point to show grooves.

4 Fill in your shell with colors and patterns. You can get ideas from these shell photos or make up your own!

Here is the hinge.

Spiral shell

Moon snails are very large and live in the ocean, but their shells are a similar shape to land snails. This moon snail shell has a spiral shape.

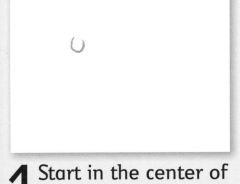

1 Start in the center of the shell and draw a curved line, as if you're drawing a circle.

2 Instead of finishing the circle, draw the line out and keep curving around and around.

3 Keep drawing until your shell is big enough. Close off the open end with a line.

If you want to add a snail, this is where its body goes!

Top tip!

Spirals are great for drawing other things such as elephant trunks or plants like ferns and vines.

4 Color in your shell. You could try straight stripes or wiggly lines.

Leaves and flowers

Plants are everywhere—in the countryside, in cities, and even in your home. Take a look at the leaves on this page. Each one has its own particular shape, color, and pattern.

All kinds of leaves

See if you can color in the other half of these leaves. Some have their outlines drawn, others have lost theirs! Can you add them in?

Use this leaf to help draw your own on the next page!

How many colors can you see in this leaf?

Sunflower

Maple

This leaf has lots of sharp points.

You can see the veins clearly on this leaf.

A wiggly line shows this wrinkled edge.

Fittonia

Lettuce

Holly

Can you finish the outline of this leaf?

Can you draw this nettle's jagged edge?

Follow the jagged lines on this bright red leaf!

Ivy

Nettle

Scarlet oak

How to draw a sunflower

Here's how to draw a bright yellow sunflower in five steps!

1 Draw the central circle. Fill with dots for the seeds.

2 Draw a first row of petals around the circle.

Each petal is two curved lines that connect at a point.

Leaves don't have to be all the same green—add some yellow or blue to your green.

3 Add petals peeking through between the front petals.

4 Add two lines for the stem, then add the leaves. Look at the sunflower leaf on page 20 to help you.

5 Now color in your sunflower!

Arranging your picture

When you arrange the parts of your drawing on the page and decide how big or small you want each object to be, you are making a composition. There are many different ways you can compose a picture.

Different compositions

Take a look at the three circles in each of the small pictures. Your pictures can look very different depending on how you arrange them.

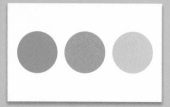

Same sizes, side by side
One simple way is to keep the objects the same size and arrange them side by side. The elephant picture follows the same composition as the circles.

Different sizes, side by side
With this composition, the circles have the same positions, but are now different sizes. In this drawing of three tents, see how this makes the smaller tents look further away.

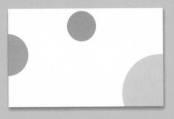

Moving off the page's edge

Not everything has to be within the edges of your paper. You can arrange some objects so they continue right off the page, like these beach balls that are flying off the page!

Large in front of small

When things are arranged one in front of the other, the front objects might cover up parts of the objects behind them. Things that are very close up are likely to go off the page, like this dinosaur here.

Try it!

Try seeing how many different compositions you can make with circles, or with anything you like!

Adding color

Colors can be used to fill in outlines and bring your drawings to life. You can choose colors to match what you see in the real world or just use your favorite colors.

Color wheel

The color wheel shows the colors you can make when you mix two different colors together. It also helps you to work out which colors are harder to mix together.

Primary colors

The three primary colors are red, yellow, and blue. All other colors can be made by mixing a combination of these three together.

Red   Yellow   Blue

Colors close to each other in the wheel are similar and easy to mix together. Yellow and orange mix to create this lighter orange.

Yellow

Orange

Red

Top tip!
Chalk and oil pastels are good for mixing colors. Use them to blend different colors together to make new ones.

24

Mixing colors

Orange, green, and purple are called secondary colors. You make them by mixing two primary colors together.

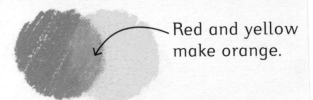

Red and yellow make orange.

Red   Yellow

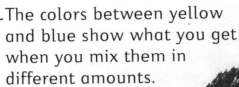

The colors between yellow and blue show what you get when you mix them in different amounts.

Blue and yellow make green.

Blue   Yellow

Red and blue make purple.

Red   Blue

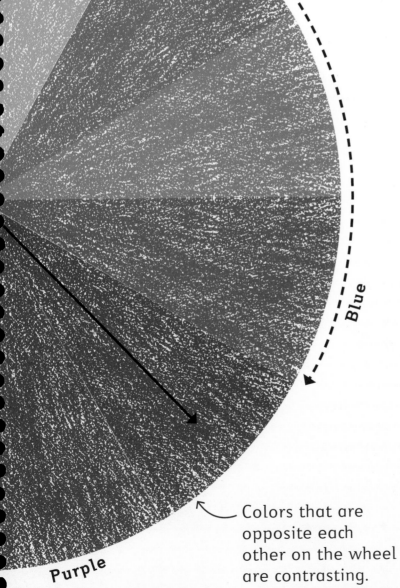

Green

Blue

Purple

Colors that are opposite each other on the wheel are contrasting.

Contrasting colors

These pairs are colors that are very different from each other. Next to each other they stand out, but if you mix them they make brown.

Red   Green

Yellow   Purple

Blue   Orange

Warm and cool colors

Different colors can create different moods in your art. You can turn a sunny picture into a stormy one just by changing the colors.

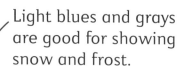

Cool colors

Blue, green, and purple are called cool colors. They remind us of things that are cold such as snow or ice.

Light blues and grays are good for showing snow and frost.

There are light and dark versions of every color. Which parts of this picture are darker?

Try it!

See how colors change your art! Fill in one scene using cool colors and the other using warm colors.

Use mostly cool colors for this picture.

You might think the sky has to be a light, cool color such as blue, but it doesn't!

Warm colors

Red, orange, and yellow are called warm colors. They remind us of things that are hot such as fire or the sun.

Rusty orange and red colors are often seen in the fall.

Top tip!

Try using different colors for the sky and clouds. They can look different depending on the weather or season.

Use mostly warm colors for this picture.

Close and far away

In real life, when you look into the distance, things look smaller the further away they are from you. The same things look bigger when they are closer to you. When you show this difference between near and far in your drawing, you are giving your work perspective.

Big and small

In this photo, you can see that the elephants vary in size depending on how near or far away they are. Look at the picture of the beach below. Can you see how the illustrator has used perspective?

Far away, elephants look very small.

This elephant is closest and looks bigger.

The horizon line is at eye level, often where land or water meets the sky.

These people are in the distance, so they are smaller and drawn further up the picture.

These people are nearer, so they are bigger and are drawn near the bottom.

28

Vanishing in the distance

Perspective is also useful to show something like a street or a train that is close to us at first but stretches away into the distance.

Up close this train looks big, but it looks thinner and thinner as it disappears into the distance.

The point where the train disappears is called the "vanishing point." Vanishing points always lie on the horizon line.

Try it!

See if you can draw a woodland scene with perspective. Draw some trees bigger and some trees smaller.

Trees that are far away should be small and about halfway down.

Trees that are closer should be big and near the bottom.

The horizon could sit somewhere here, above your most distant trees.

How to draw a landscape

A landscape is a picture of an outdoor scene, such as a park or forest. Here is one way to draw a landscape. In the scene there is a house, trees, and a road leading to mountains in the distance.

Top tip!
Landscapes don't always have to be in the countryside. You can try drawing a city scene instead.

1 Begin by drawing the tree that is closest to you. This will look bigger than the others.

2 Draw the house using a rectangle for the door and squares for the windows. Add a slanted roof.

Horizon line

3 Place the horizon line in the distance, then add a road that narrows as it reaches it.

4 Draw mountains on the horizon. Add more trees, getting smaller the further up the page they are.

5 Now you can add your own details, such as clouds, the sun, a plane, or a train.

The horizon is at eye level, often where the land meets the sky.

6 Fill in your picture with colors and textures. The ground could have a grassy texture and the trees could be leafy.

How to draw a boat

Here you can see how to draw a boat using just a few simple lines. Once you've got the basic boat shape, you can have fun adding details to create your very own boat scene.

1 Start with two curved lines for the top edge of the boat. Then draw two short curves down for the sides. You don't need to draw the bottom, because this will be in the water!

2 Draw a gentle wavy line to show the water hiding the bottom of the boat. Continue the line beyond the edges of the boat.

3 For the mast, draw two straight lines close together, going up from the boat, then join them at the top. Add a curved triangle for the sail. Add stripes if you wish!

4 Draw a line above your boat in the water—this is the horizon line, where the water meets the sky. Add a few more wavy lines for ripples. Add details such as clouds, birds, or an island to your scene!

5 Now have fun adding color to your scene. Decorate your boat and sail. This sail is stripy, but you may want to add dots or even flowers.

Top tip!
For bigger, choppier waves use more wiggly lines. Use flatter, horizontal lines for smooth, gentle waves.

Blend different colors for the sea and sky—they don't have to be just blue!

Shading

When you look at something in real life, the parts of it in shadow can look darker than the parts in the light. You can show this in your drawings by adding shading.

Black and white

All colors have light and dark shades, or tones. Here is an example of the tones from black to white.

Black is the darkest.

Gray is a medium tone, in between black and white.

White is the lightest.

3-D Shading

Using shading can make your drawings look three-dimensional (3-D). This means that your picture has depth, instead of looking flat.

Photograph

The egg looks lighter where there's more light shining on it.

Flat outline

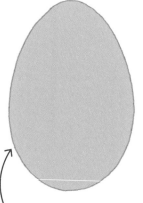

Without light and dark shading, the egg looks flat.

Drawn with shading

Adding shading makes the egg look rounded.

34

Light and dark colors

A color can look very different depending on its tone. Here you can see light and dark tones in green and blue.

 **Photograph**

 **Drawn with shading**

Notice where the blue gets lighter and darker.

You can use darker blues for shading or even another color, such as dark purple.

Making marks

If you fill in an outline solidly with black, you make a flat, black shape. But if you fill it with lots of small marks instead, you can add depth by making some areas lighter, some darker.

Hatching

Drawing lots of small lines that all go in a similar direction is called hatching.

Crosshatching

Drawing lots of small lines crisscrossing over each other is called crosshatching and can create a darker effect than hatching.

Stippling

Drawing lots of little dots is called stippling. Use more dots for shaded areas and fewer, or no dots, for light areas.

How to draw a 3-D mug

Have you ever had a mug of hot chocolate on a cold day? How does the shape of the mug feel in your hands? Now try to draw a 3-D mug using shading.

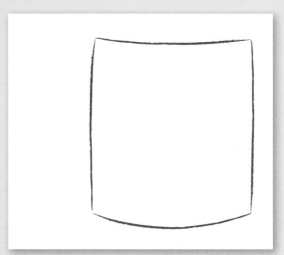
Top tip!
Change the shape and sides of your mug to draw other objects such as vases, bowls, or buckets.

1 Draw two straight lines for the sides of the mug.

2 Add the top and bottom. These lines are almost flat, but curve downward a little.

3 Draw a curve that goes slightly upward at the top to show the other edge of the mug. Add lines for the handle.

4 Add shading for the parts of the mug that are in shadow. You could try crisscrossing lines to make it darker.

This lamp shows the direction that the light is coming from.

This mug has a tiny shadow underneath it.

5 Now add shading to the handle. Try adding a little shadow under the mug. This should be very dark.

Adding color

You can shade with color instead of marks. You can also try adding colorful patterns such as dots, squares, or flowers.

Pastels are great for shading. You can smudge them to go from light to dark.

Try adding a spotty pattern to your mug.

Drawing animals

Animals come in all different shapes and sizes, and there are many ways to draw them. You could start by outlining your animal, or begin with shapes like circles, or draw details like the eyes and nose first.

Try drawing the outline of the whole duck, before you add detail.

Duck

Starting with ovals and circles helps give your animal a shape.

Kangaroo

Dog

How about starting with the most detailed part of your drawing—the face?

Try drawing the hippo yourself after you've practiced the circles here!

Try it!

We've drawn the first two ovals on the hippo. Can you draw the ones for the body and legs?

How to draw a dog's face

Sometimes it's easiest to draw an animal's face one detail at a time. The nose and eyes are a good place to start.

Top tip!
Many animals have similar faces or bodies. Patterns, colors, and texture on their skin or fur help tell them apart.

1 Start with an oval for the face, then add the nose.

2 Draw a curved line up from the nose. Add circles for the eyes on either side.

3 Draw three curves underneath the nose to make the mouth.

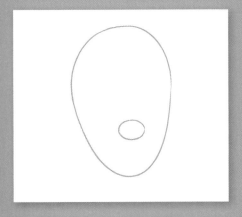

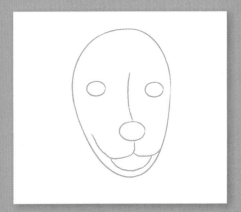

Add details like nostrils, teeth, and shiny eyes.

4 Add the ears. Fill in the outline of the face, making it wider on the left and narrower on the right.

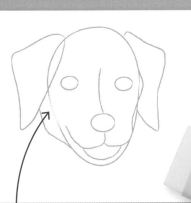

Erase the first oval.

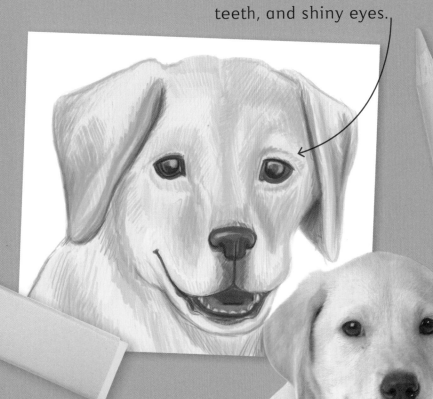

You can add furry texture or just color it in!

39

How to draw a cat

A cat might seem tricky to draw, but if you use simple shapes to guide you, you can draw one quite easily. Here you can see how to draw a cat in six easy steps.

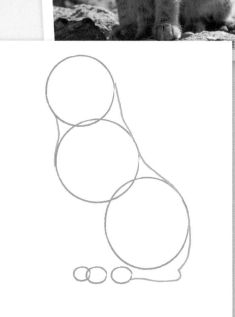

Press lightly because these circles will be erased later.

1 With a pencil, draw a circle for the cat's head. Add two circles for the body and three small ovals for the paws.

2 With a colored pencil, draw around the outer edges of the circles to make the outline of the cat's body.

Muzzle

3 Draw three lines for the front legs leading to the two left paws. Add a small circle in pencil for the cat's muzzle.

Rub out the gray pencil lines.

Add two triangle shapes for the ears.

4 Trace over the head, muzzle, and paws with a colored pencil and add short lines for the toes. Draw the tail.

5 Draw the nose, then three curves underneath it for the mouth. Add two ovals with a small oval in each for the eyes. Whiskers are a few gentle lines.

6 Now it's time to color in your cat! This one is ginger and has green eyes.

For the cat's fur, try drawing vertical or slanted lines with colored pencils.

Use different colors to draw any cat you like!

Top tip!

For smooth fur, draw lots of short lines close together. You can make lines longer and curvier for fluffier cats!

How to draw a parrot

Parrots can fly high in the sky, swooping and soaring with their brightly colored wings. Here is one way of drawing a type of parrot, called a macaw.

A macaw

Instead of using shapes to draw the body, try starting with the details on the bird's face and building up from there.

Parrots don't have long necks so just go straight from the head to the body.

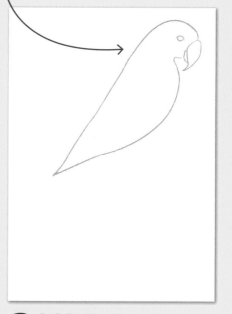

1 Draw the beak and add the eye so it is level with the middle of it. The beak on a parrot droops down close to the face.

2 Add the head, curving from the top and bottom of the beak. Carry on with the body, coming to a point at its back.

The wings fold over the parrot's long tail.

3 Draw the parrot's feet, then add in the branch underneath.

4 Add lines for the wings and outline the long, pointy tail feathers.

5 Now get creative! Fill your bird with color and use patterns to show feather textures.

Top tip!

Feathers near the head are so small you can't see them separately. They get larger in the wings, and longest in the tail.

Try decorating your background with tropical flowers and plants!

How to draw a horse

Horses are tricky to draw but starting with circles can make it easier. Look at the way a horse walks and trots. You can try moving your horse's legs into different positions to show how they move.

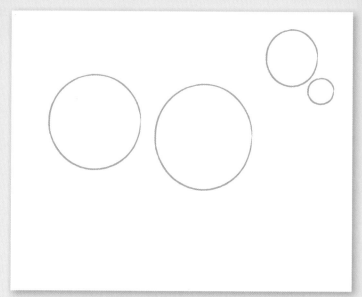

1 Use a pencil to draw two circles for the horse's head. Draw two larger circles for the body.

2 Draw lines around the circles to give the horse shape. Leave space at the bottom for the legs.

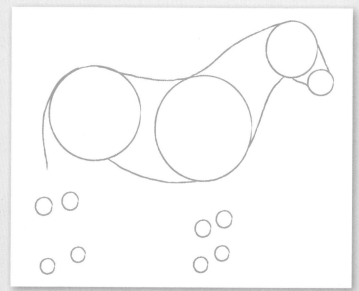

3 Draw circles for the knees and ankles. Space them out to make the legs long.

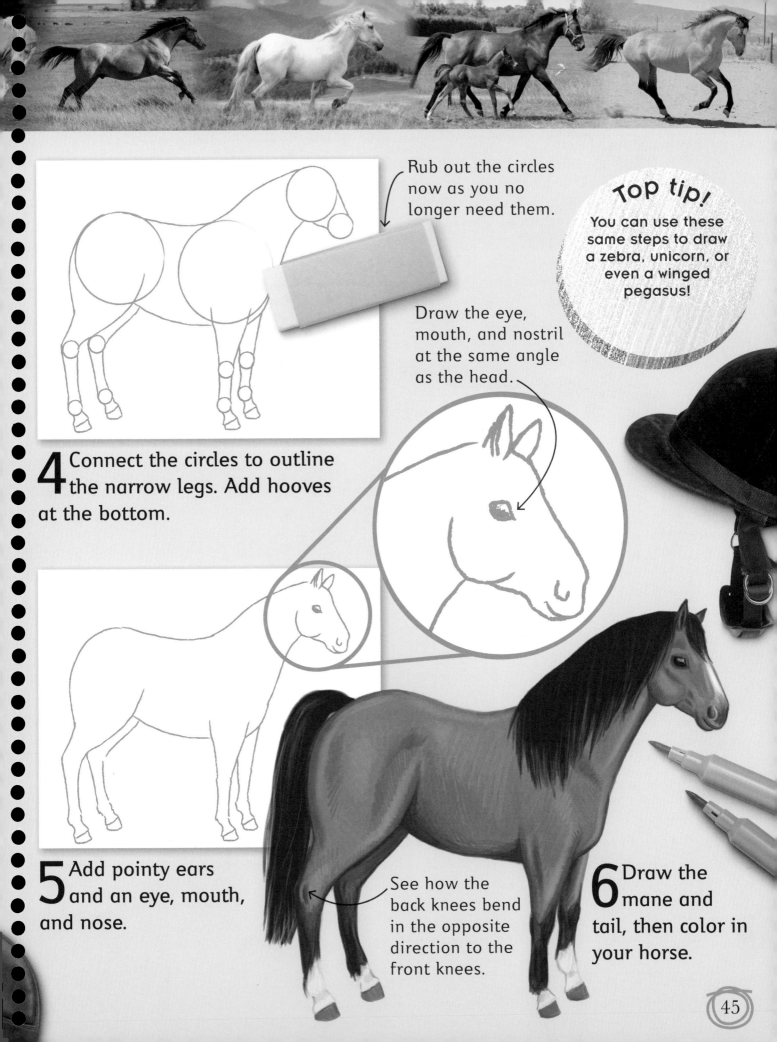

Rub out the circles now as you no longer need them.

Top tip! You can use these same steps to draw a zebra, unicorn, or even a winged pegasus!

Draw the eye, mouth, and nostril at the same angle as the head.

4 Connect the circles to outline the narrow legs. Add hooves at the bottom.

5 Add pointy ears and an eye, mouth, and nose.

See how the back knees bend in the opposite direction to the front knees.

6 Draw the mane and tail, then color in your horse.

45

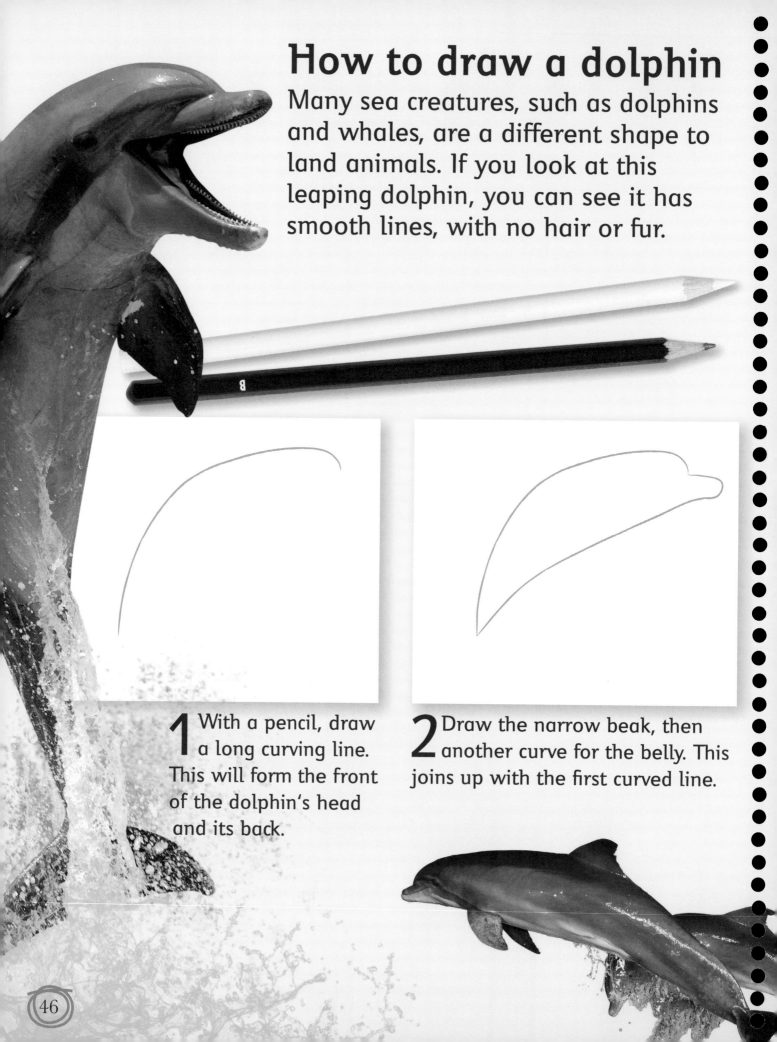

How to draw a dolphin

Many sea creatures, such as dolphins and whales, are a different shape to land animals. If you look at this leaping dolphin, you can see it has smooth lines, with no hair or fur.

1 With a pencil, draw a long curving line. This will form the front of the dolphin's head and its back.

2 Draw the narrow beak, then another curve for the belly. This joins up with the first curved line.

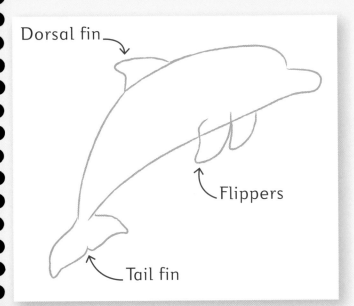

Dorsal fin

Flippers

Tail fin

3 Add a curvy triangle for the dorsal fin on the dolphin's back. Draw two flippers and then add the tail fin at the pointed end.

4 Erase the extra lines from the dorsal fin, tail fin, and flipper. Add a line for the forehead, then draw an eye and a smiley mouth!

5 Now you can color in your dolphin and add splashy water. If you want to, you can try adding a horizon line in the distance and wiggly lines for waves.

Try it!

You can follow the same steps to draw an orca, or killer whale. Use this photo to help you with the lines and colors.

Using grids

When you find an image that you like, you might want to copy it and create your own picture. Using a grid helps you to break down the details of a picture, so you can copy it square by square.

Drawing a grid

A grid has been drawn over the top of this picture, dividing it into small sections.

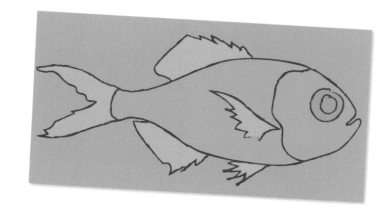

Look at the image to see how detailed it is.

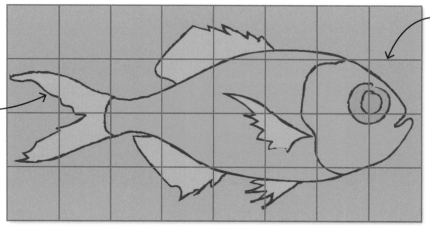

The grid breaks up the picture that is being copied.

This grid has been drawn in pencil so it can be erased when the picture is finished.

This grid has the same number of squares as the one above.

Each square is copied one at a time.

48

Copying the picture

Here is a picture of an elephant with a grid drawn over the top. Look at how the elephant is placed in the grid. Which part of the elephant is in each square?

Your grid should have the same number of squares as the one you are copying. This grid is six squares high and five squares wide.

Use a ruler to measure your grid and keep all the lines straight.

Draw the outlines one square at a time. Erase the grid before filling it in with color.

Stegosaurus square by square

Here is a picture of a stegosaurus stomping through the undergrowth. Copy the picture in the grid made for you below. How does it feel to draw square by square?

top tip!
You can make your picture bigger or smaller by drawing a grid that has larger or smaller squares.

Check how far up or down in its square each part of your drawing is.

Some squares will be completely empty.

See how the volcano starts in this square, but continues into the ones nearby.

Notice how much of the square each detail fills up.

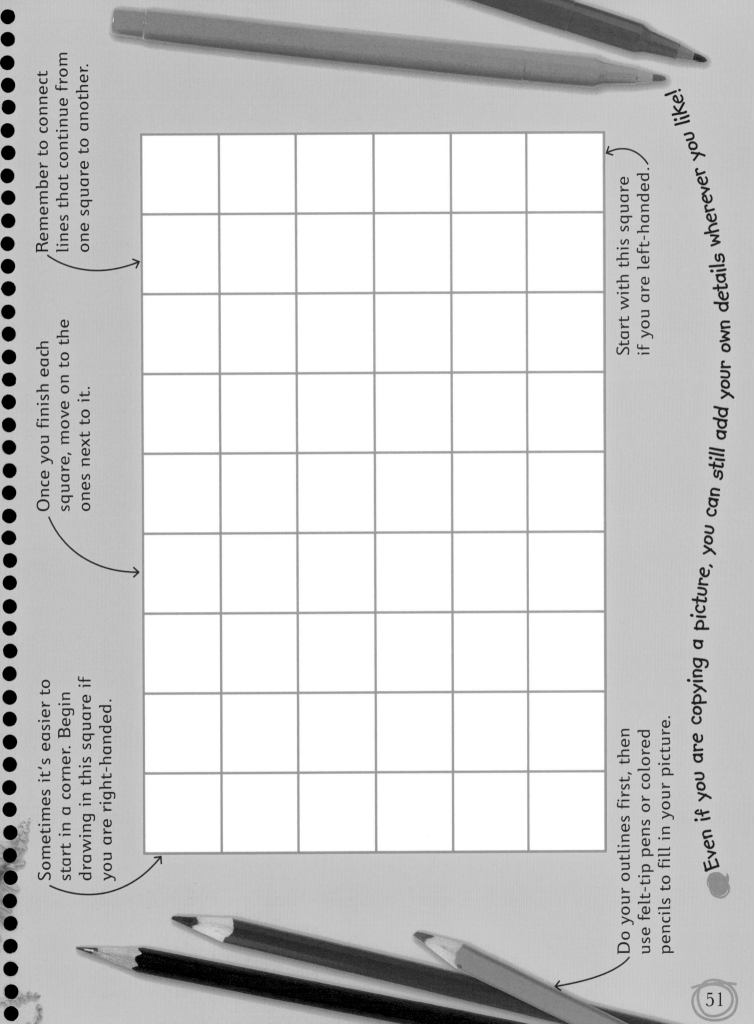

Remember to connect lines that continue from one square to another.

Once you finish each square, move on to the ones next to it.

Start with this square if you are left-handed.

Sometimes it's easier to start in a corner. Begin drawing in this square if you are right-handed.

Do your outlines first, then use felt-tip pens or colored pencils to fill in your picture.

Even if you are copying a picture, you can still add your own details wherever you like!

Underwater scene

Make your own grid to copy this underwater scene with sharks, a shipwreck, and even treasure!

Measuring your grid

To copy this scene, first you need to draw a grid over the top of it. Follow these steps to make the grid using a pencil and ruler.

1 Draw a box around the picture.

2 Use a ruler to measure along the sides, evenly dividing the picture.

3 Use a ruler to draw lines that join up the marks and make boxes.

Join these lines together to complete the grid.

Try it!

Use this space to make a grid, identical to the one above, then copy the picture inside.

Copy the picture, one box at a time.

Think of fun sea creatures and treasures to add to your underwater shipwreck!

How to draw a face

A portrait is a picture of a person's face. Here is how to draw a portrait, showing where to place the eyes, nose, mouth, and ears. You could draw a self-portrait (a portrait of yourself) or a picture of a friend!

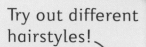
Try out different hairstyles!

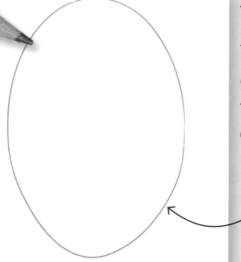

1 Draw an oval for the outline of the face. Depending on the shape of the face, it might be rounder, longer, or have a pointier chin.

Press lightly as you may change your mind about the shape later.

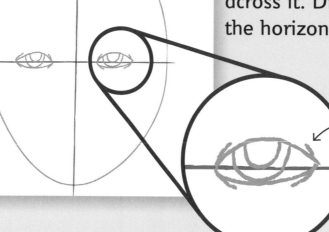

2 Draw a vertical line down the center of the oval and a horizontal line across it. Draw the eyes on the horizontal line.

Don't forget details such as the pupils and eyelids.

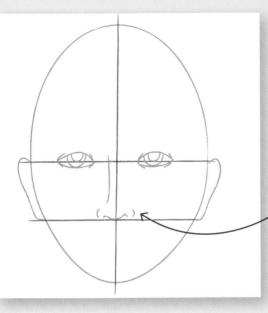

3 Draw another horizontal line between the eyes and chin. Draw the nose and ears between these two lines.

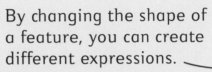

The bottom of the nose is the main part we see.

By changing the shape of a feature, you can create different expressions.

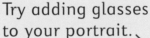

4 Add one more horizontal line between the nose and chin. Draw the lips as curves up and down from this line.

Try adding glasses to your portrait.

5 Add eyebrows, hair, and a neck.

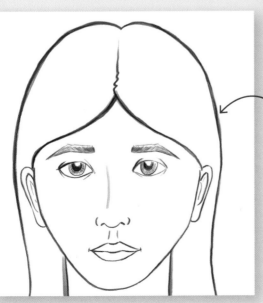

Erase the guide lines before adding color.

Top tip!
Colors add details to your person's face. There are many different colors for skin tones, hair, lips, and eyes.

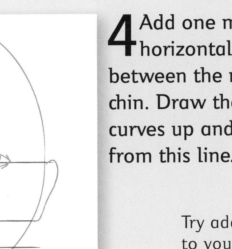

Artists often use wooden models to help them draw people.

These shapes give you the basic outline of the person.

Real people might be bigger, thinner, taller, or shorter. These shapes are just to get started.

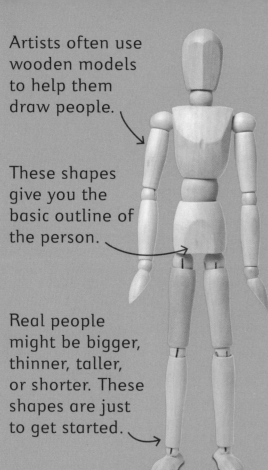

How to draw a person

There are lots of different ways to draw a person. Try these steps to draw a person using simple shapes. Think about which parts of the body connect together and where the joints are.

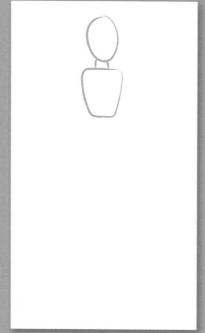

1 Draw an oval for the face, then add the neck and chest underneath.

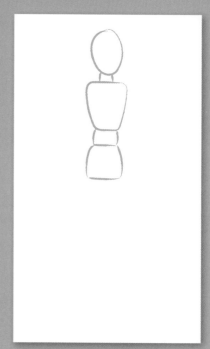

2 Add a square for the hips. Draw two lines to connect the hips with the chest.

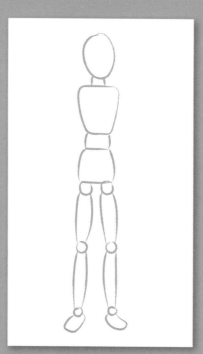

3 The legs come down from the hips. Draw circles for the joints, such as ankles. Add the feet.

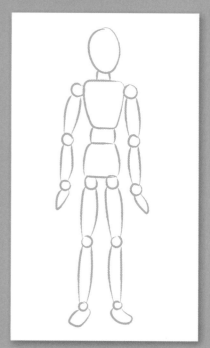

4 Draw the arms with circles for the shoulders, elbows, and wrists. The hands end below the hips.

Changing positions

You can draw your figure walking, running, or in any position you choose. The circles show you where the joints can bend.

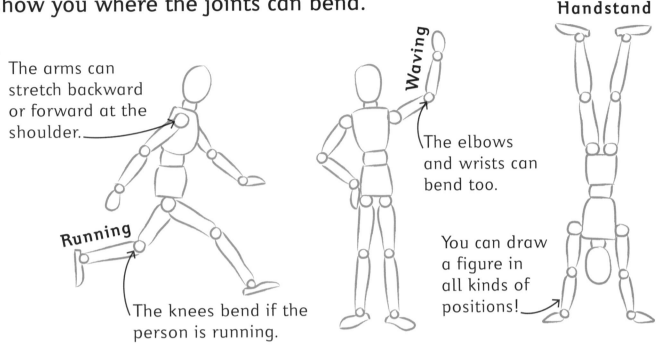

The arms can stretch backward or forward at the shoulder.

Running

The knees bend if the person is running.

Waving

Handstand

The elbows and wrists can bend too.

You can draw a figure in all kinds of positions!

Clothes

Once you've drawn the basic shapes, you can draw outlines over your person to show their clothes, hair, skin, and face.

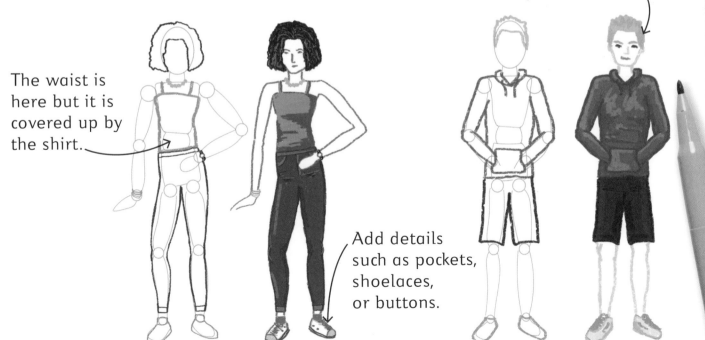

You can try different hairstyles and faces.

The waist is here but it is covered up by the shirt.

Add details such as pockets, shoelaces, or buttons.

You could try drawing someone you know or even an imaginary person.

Using photographs

Photographs are great for drawing from. They're very useful for giving the overall shape of something, showing details, and for getting ideas.

Looking for outlines

We use outlines to show the shape of what we're drawing. Look at this photo. Can you see what kinds of outlines you would use for each object?

What kind of line would you use for jagged mountains like these?

What shapes would you use for balloons? Which parts are curved? Which parts are pointy?

Try smudgy dots and dashes for grass and flowers.

Picking and choosing

You don't have to draw everything in the photo. Pick and choose what you like or what you find useful, and focus on that.

Try putting your favorite detail from a photo into a scene you've made up.

58

Try it!

Try drawing from these photos. One is outlined for you to color in and shade. Use the other to copy outlines and textures, adding any colors or details you like!

Setting up a still life

A still life is a drawing or painting that is based on a specially arranged group of objects. The still life below groups together oranges and a glass of orange juice. You can try making your own still life at home.

Arrange your objects carefully before you start.

Can you see where the oranges are lighter or darker?

What kind of shapes do you see? How big is each part?

Where are edges curved or straight?

Still-life drawing is a great way to practice shading!

Pastels let you blend colors smoothly and draw quickly.

Drawing from real life

You can make fantastic drawings based on the things you see every day. You might sketch a tree or a flower, draw your best friend or pet, or make a still life out of objects in your home, such as flowers, fruit, or even your favorite toys!

Top tip!
You don't need to draw absolutely everything in detail. It's fine to just focus on one part that you like the best!

If there is lots of movement around you, such as leaves blowing in the wind, use fast, active movements with your hand.

See how you can draw the basics of this bike with just a few strokes, instead of drawing every detail.

If you don't have much time, you can outline the basics first and fill in more detail later, at home.

Drawing outside

It can be great fun to get outside and draw something quickly, capturing the moment of what you are drawing. You can show a whole scene, or just focus on one thing.

Silhouettes

When you can see the outline of something clearly, but everything inside its edges looks black, we say it's "in silhouette." Silhouettes happen in real life as well as in art.

How they happen

Silhouettes happen when it's quite dark outside, often at sunset or sunrise. The sun casts a brighter light behind the thing you're looking at.

It's difficult to see the details in this silhouette of a ship, but its edges are illuminated by the setting sun behind it.

Portrait silhouettes

Portrait silhouettes show unique facial features clearly. The person has to be drawn from the side (in profile).

Portrait silhouettes were made by artists before photographs existed!

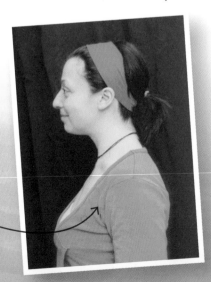

Portrait silhouettes can be traced from a photograph and then the outline filled in.

Silhouetted scene

You can use silhouettes to create atmospheric, dramatic scenes using any art materials you like.

If you're using messy materials such as chalk or pastels, color the sky and then draw your black silhouettes over the top. If you start with the black it might smear.

Chalk is great for blending colors in the sky.

You could use charcoal for the silhouettes.

Try it!

Make your own sunset scene. The silhouettes could be of a house, tree, person, animal, city skyline, or whatever you'd like to try!

Drawing spaceships

You can draw from real life or from your imagination, or from both! Use these steps to draw a spaceship. What do you imagine it will look like and who will be flying it? Will it be a spacecraft sent from Earth or from an alien planet?

1 Start with a basic shape for the spaceship body. Here we have used an oval but you could try any shape you like.

2 Start drawing details. This spaceship has a large, round window on the top and rockets on the bottom.

3 Now add smaller details such as extra windows, landing gear, or flames on the rockets. Then add a background and color.

Try it!

Use this space to draw your own spaceship. Where will it be flying to?

Top tip!

Black paper is great for showing the night sky. Draw stars and planets by pressing firmly using chalk or oil pastels.

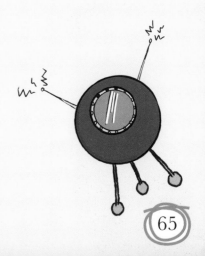

How to draw a dragon

Dragons have appeared in stories and art for thousands of years. Sometimes they are deadly enemies and other times they are helpful friends. Follow these steps to draw your own dragon.

1 In pencil, draw circles for the body, knees, feet, face, and snout. Connect them all with lines and draw a wavy line for the tail.

2 Draw around your shapes for the dragon's head, body, legs, feet, and tail.

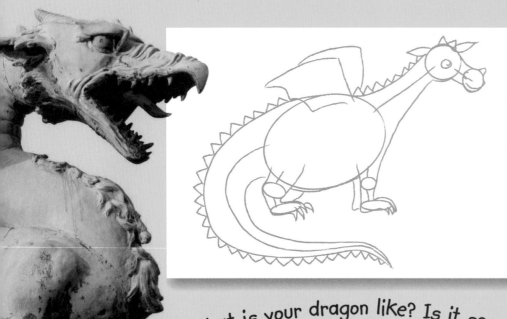

3 Give your dragon an eye and some ears. It could also have wings and spiky plates down its back. What details would you like your dragon to have?

What is your dragon like? Is it scary, friendly, or funny?

4 Erase the lines you don't need. Fill in some more details such as horns and patterns on its wings.

Top tip!
Drawing your dragon so that it goes off the page makes it look bigger and more dramatic!

Chinese dragons are celebrated for their power and strength.

5 Color in your dragon and add in a background if you want to. Maybe your dragon is guarding precious treasure!

Telling a story

Pictures can be used to tell stories. You can illustrate a favorite story or poem, or a story you make up yourself! Here are some ideas to get you started.

Characters

Who or what is the story about? Who are the main characters and what do they look like?

Pirate

Princess

Astronaut

Monster

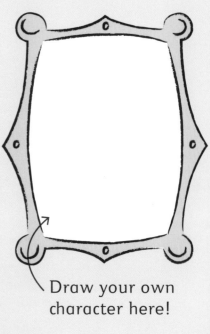

Draw your own character here!

Setting

Where and when would you like your story to be set? In a castle long ago or a modern-day city? What's the weather like?

Castle

The moon

Ship

City

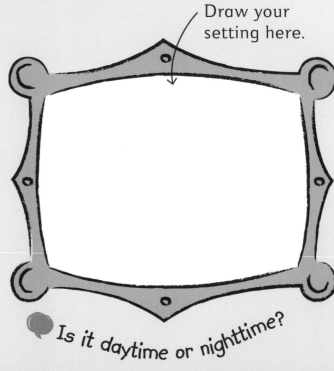

Draw your setting here.

Is it daytime or nighttime?

68

Try it!

Use the box to illustrate this princess story in one scene!

The princess is riding her horse toward the castle to rescue her brother from a fire-breathing dragon!

Now try illustrating your own scene based on your character from the previous page, or make up a new one! You can tell the story in one picture, or divide the box up into different scenes.

Cartoons

Cartoons tell stories in pictures, which are often funny. The characters are usually drawn with strong, simple lines that exaggerate certain features. A person who draws cartoons is called a cartoonist.

Top tip!

Characters need to look the same in each box, so it's best to keep the features simple and easy to copy!

Comic strips are made up of several cartoon drawings that tell a story one box at a time, sometimes with no speech, like this one.

Cartoon symbols

Cartoonists use symbols for showing how a character is speaking or moving. The way speech bubbles are shaped suggests different things.

Speech bubble

Words go inside the bubbles!

Action sounds

BOOM!

Thought bubble

I think I'd like to draw a cartoon!

Whisper bubble

Pssst, come here!

Short lines around a figure make it look like it's shaking.

Lines behind add speed to a running figure.

70

Try it!

Try making your own comic strip! You can use one or all of these characters, or create your own. Make up your own story and add speech bubbles and action sounds!

Use bright felt-tips to color in your comic strip!

Adapting your drawings

When you begin drawing you might have a certain picture in your mind. However, as you add to your drawing it can turn into something new. Here are a few ways of adapting, or changing, your pictures.

Photograph of a butterfly

Changing the picture

These four drawings of a butterfly are all based on the photo above, but each one looks quite different.

You might draw a pencil sketch of the butterfly.

You might copy the photo using similar colors.

You might add a colorful background to your butterfly.

You might decide to keep the same outline, but change the colors.

Abstract art

An abstract drawing is one that doesn't look realistic. However, the idea may have come from something real.

This abstract drawing was inspired by the shape and colors of a butterfly.

Try it!

Do you have any drawings that you would like to adapt? Use this space to practice changing an image. You could try adding color or breaking up its shape to make it more abstract.

73

Digital tools

Many things that can be drawn with a pen or pencil can also be drawn using digital tools on a computer. Digital-drawing programs help you create hundreds of different effects and using them can be faster than drawing by hand.

Photograph of a beetle

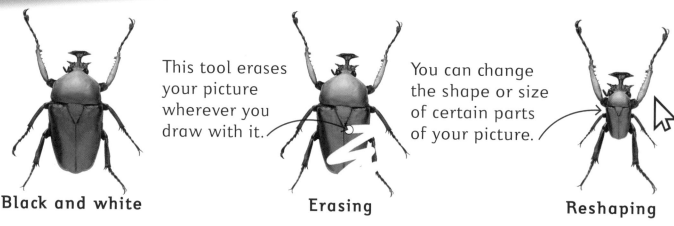

Black and white

This tool erases your picture wherever you draw with it.

Erasing

You can change the shape or size of certain parts of your picture.

Reshaping

Changing colors

The color of this beetle has been changed using a digital program. This has made one image into lots of different pictures.

You can use digital tools to quickly fill areas of your image with solid color.

Tracing and changing

Digital tools can make marks that look the same as real art materials. Digital tools can be used to trace lines from a photo and then fill them in like a drawing. This can make them look as if they were drawn by hand.

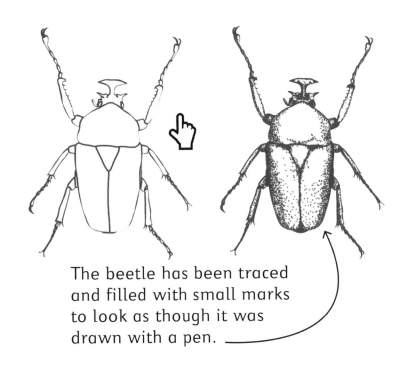

The beetle has been traced and filled with small marks to look as though it was drawn with a pen.

Patterns and copying

When using a computer you can make exact copies of images and then change their color and size. You can even make new designs by repeating an image over and over like a pattern.

Top tip!

Many phones and tablets have digital drawing apps that you can use to sketch ideas when you're not at home.

You can print digital images onto paper or even onto T-shirts!

Drawing as a job

If you are an illustrator, cartoonist, or artist, drawing is central to your job. But many other people use drawing as an important part of their job, too.

Architecture

Architects design buildings by making detailed drawings of what each part will look like. Traditionally, these were drawn by hand, but today it is often done with computers.

Fashion design

Fashion designers draw sketches of clothing to show how it will look when it is made. They create new styles and fashion ideas.

Scientific illustration

Scientific illustrators draw detailed pictures of things in nature, like animals and plants. They explain parts of science that aren't easily shown through photographs. This is great for learning about the insides of things, such as the human body.

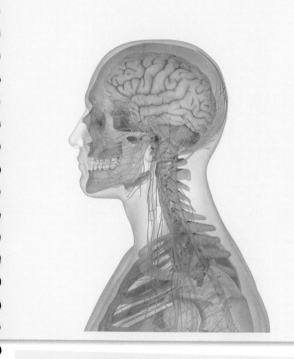

Storyboarding

Filmmakers use storyboards to plan their films. A storyboard is a series of drawings that show what each scene will look like.

Car design

Car designers develop ideas for new cars. Their drawings show the style of a car and explain how it will work.

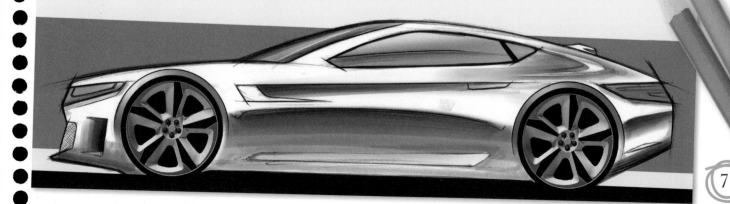

Keeping a sketchbook

You can keep a sketchbook to draw what you see around you. Record your ideas, thoughts, observations, and memories in your book. Draw from real life or from your imagination!

Top tip!

A small sketchbook is easier to take on long trips. You can always draw more when you get home!

Sketchbook

Sketchbooks are made of blank drawing paper and come in different sizes. The paper can be thick or thin, smooth or rough.

Quick sketches are great for practicing, and you can fill in details later.

Crosshatching and stippling are great for shading.

You can make leaf rubbings using a wax crayon.

If you don't have colors with you, just add them when you get home.

You can use any drawing tools you like, but pens, pencils, and colored pencils are easy to carry.

Whole scene

Use your sketchbook for any kind of drawing! You can make rough sketches or finished drawings that fill a whole page.

Charcoal is great for adding shading.

Famous sketches

Artists throughout history have used sketchbooks to practice techniques and plan their art. Some drew in pencil, while others used ink, charcoal, and even paint.

French artist Edgar Degas made pencil sketches of ballerinas to practice for larger paintings.

You could use the following blank pages as your own sketchbook!

79

DK | Penguin Random House

Senior Editor Marie Greenwood
Editor Katy Lennon
US Editor Rebecca Warren
Project Art Editor Hoa Luc
Designer Emma Hobson
Jacket Coordinator Francesca Young
Jacket Designer Amy Keast
Managing Editor Laura Gilbert
Managing Art Editor Diane Peyton Jones
Pre-production Nikoleta Parasaki
Production Manager Pankaj Sharma
Picture Reseach Rob Nunn, Aditya Katyal
Producer Srijana Gurung
Art Director Martin Wilson
Publisher Sarah Larter
Publishing Director Sophie Mitchell

Illustrator Katie Knutton
Additional Illustration Emma Hobson

First American Edition, 2017
Published in the United States by DK Publishing
1745 Broadway, 20th Floor, New York, NY 10019

Copyright © 2017 Dorling Kindersley Limited.
DK, a Division of Penguin Random House LLC
22 23 24 25 26 12 11 10 9 8
014–298505–Feb/2017

All rights reserved.
Without limiting the rights under the copyright reserved above, no part of this publication may be reproduced, stored in or introduced into a retrieval system, or transmitted, in any form, or by any means (electronic, mechanical, photocopying, recording, or otherwise), without the prior written permission of the copyright owner.
Published in Great Britain by Dorling Kindersley Limited

A catalog record for this book
is available from the Library of Congress.
ISBN: 978-1-4654-5685-4

DK books are available at special discounts when purchased in bulk for sales promotions, premiums, fund-raising, or educational use. For details, contact: DK Publishing Special Markets, 1745 Broadway, 20th Floor, New York, NY 10019
SpecialSales@dk.com

Printed and bound in China

For the curious
www.dk.com

MIX
Paper | Supporting responsible forestry
FSC www.fsc.org FSC™ C018179

This book was made with Forest Stewardship Council™ certified paper–one small step in DK's commitment to a sustainable future. For more information go to www.dk.com/our-green-pledge

The publisher would like to thank Polly Goodman for proofreading, Jemma Battaglia, Yasmin Mokha, Kiran Kheradia, and Leah Panigada-Carey for additional illustration and Andy Crawford for photography.

The publisher would like to thank the following for their kind permission to reproduce their photographs:

(Key: a-above; b-below/bottom; c-center; f-far; l-left; r-right; t-top)

11 Dreamstime.com: Jxpfeer (cla). **Thomas Marent:** Thomas Marent (clb). **12-13 Dreamstime.com:** Lawcain (b). **13 Alamy Stock Photo:** Danita Delimont (br). **14 123RF.com:** Pedro Antonio SalaverrÃ¬a Calahorra (c). **Alamy Stock Photo:** ableimages (cra); Image Source (cb). **Thomas Marent:** (cr). **19 123RF.com:** Petra Schüller (tl). **20 123RF.com:** Maggie Molloy (bc); Dmitriy Syechin (ca); Taiga (c). **26 Dreamstime.com:** Roxana Gonzalez / Rgbspace (cr). **27 Dreamstime.com:** Roxana Gonzalez / Rgbspace (cl). **28 Alamy Stock Photo:** Yadid Levy (cr). **29 Getty Images:** Laurence Labat / Corbis Documentary (cl). **31 Dreamstime.com:** Rostislav Glinsky (br); Valentyn Shevchenko (bl). **Getty Images:** Saswato Chowdhury / EyeEm (bc). **32 Alamy Stock Photo:** Feng Yu (bc). **Dorling Kindersley:** Alex Wilson / RNLI - Royal National Lifeboat Institute (bl). **33 Alamy Stock Photo:** MISCELLANEOUSTOCK (cr); Feng Yu (cra). **37 Dorling Kindersley:** Gary Ombler / Burgess Dorling and Leigh (cra). **38 123RF.com:** smileus (cl). **Fotolia:** Eric Isselee (br). **40 Alamy Stock Photo:** Claudia Holzförster (tr). **42 Fotolia:** Elena Blokhina (bl). **44 123RF.com:** Viktoria Makarova (ftl, tc); John Young (ftr). **Dorling Kindersley:** Stephen Oliver (clb). **Dreamstime.com:** Viktoria Makarova (tl). **45 123RF.com:** Stefan Petru Andronache (tl); M.G. Mooij (tc). **Dreamstime.com:** Rebecca Hermanson (ftl); Mark Liedel (ftr). **46 Getty Images:** Stephen Frink (l). **47 Alamy Stock Photo:** blickwinkel / Schmidbauer (crb). **50 Fotolia:** Elena Blokhina (tl). **54 123RF.com:** subbotina (clb); Vitaly Valua / domenicogelermo (tr). **55 123RF.com:** maridav (cra). **Dreamstime.com:** Rixie (br). **58 Dreamstime.com:** Elenatur (c). **59 Dorling Kindersley:** David Peart (crb). **Fotolia:** Stephen Sweet (cla). **60 Alamy Stock Photo:** Valentyn Volkov (tr). **61 123RF.com:** just_regress (Grass). **62 Jamie Marshall:** (cr). **64 NASA:** JPL (bl). **64-65 Getty Images:** John Davis / Stocktrek Images (Background). **66 Dorling Kindersley:** Richard Leeney / Bergen County, NJ, Law and Public Safety Institute (tr); Stephen Oliver (cr). **67 Dorling Kindersley:** Richard Leeney / Bergen County, NJ, Law and Public Safety Institute (bl); Stephen Oliver (tl). **78 Alamy Stock Photo:** Art Directors & TRIP (cb); Nature Photographers Ltd (clb); Michael Burrell (Notebook). **79 Alamy Stock Photo:** Art Reserve (b)

All other images © Dorling Kindersley.
For further information see: www.dkimages.com